PUFFIN BOOKS
RANI LAKSHMIBAI

Sonia Mehta is a children's writer who believes that sparking off a child's imagination opens up a world of adventure. She has been writing for children for over two decades. Her body of work is wide-ranging—she created one of India's first dedicated children's newspaper sections; conceptualized the *Cadbury Bournvita Quiz Contest* for TV; and has written books, songs, poems and stories for leading publishers in India, several African nations, the USA and the UK.

She lives in Mumbai and runs Quadrum Solutions, a content company she co-founded. She is also the co-founder of PodSquad, a retail children's edutainment brand that firmly believes that children learn best when they are having fun.

Most days, Sonia can be found pounding away at her computer—when she is not playing with her dachshunds, the two little loves of her life.

Read More in the Junior Lives Series

Mother Teresa
Mahatma Gandhi

Rani Lakshmibai

Sonia Mehta

Illustrated by Jitendra Mahadik

PUFFIN BOOKS

An imprint of Penguin Random House

PUFFIN BOOKS

USA | Canada | UK | Ireland | Australia
New Zealand | India | South Africa | China | Singapore

Puffin Books is part of the Penguin Random House group of companies
whose addresses can be found at global.penguinrandomhouse.com

Published by Penguin Random House India Pvt. Ltd
4th Floor, Capital Tower 1, MG Road,
Gurugram 122 002, Haryana, India

Penguin
Random House
India

First published in Puffin Books by Penguin Random House India 2018

Text and illustrations copyright © Quadrum Solutions Pvt. Ltd 2018
Series copyright © Penguin Random House India 2018

ISBN 9780143428251

Design and layout by Quadrum Solutions Pvt. Ltd

Printed at Manipal Technologies Limited, India

www.penguin.co.in

MIX
Paper | Supporting
responsible forestry
FSC® C043100

Contents

Contents

1 A Little Tomboy

The little girl was nowhere to be found. Her aunt had searched for her everywhere. There were peas to be shelled, rice to be cleaned and a lot of housework waiting to be completed.

Suddenly, the aunt heard the little girl's voice wafting from the street outside. She looked out of the window and saw the child playing seven tiles with some boys.

'Manu!' her aunt called. 'Come in at once. There is much work to be done in the house.'

'I won't,' the girl replied defiantly. 'I want to play. Why should I have to work while my friends play outside?'

Her aunt didn't know then—and nor did the girl's poor unsuspecting father—that the motherless young girl would grow up to become Rani Lakshmibai, the queen of Jhansi. She would become famous all over the world for her bravery and for the way she fought for her kingdom against an entire army of British soldiers.

Fearless Manu

Rani Lakshmibai wasn't born a princess. In fact, she was born in a simple Brahmin family. Her father's name was Moropant Tambe and her mother was Bhagirathi Bai. People are not sure about exactly which year she was born, but it was probably around 1827, in Kashi (now the city of Varanasi), and she was named Manikarnika. But everyone knew her as Manu.

When Rani Lakshmibai was a little girl, she was a complete tomboy. She didn't behave

> **Did You Know?**
> Manikarnika means one with jewelled ears. It is also the name of a river in India.

like other little girls. Instead of playing with dolls, she loved to run around and play all kinds of outdoor games. Her dearest wish was to ride an elephant—like she had seen men do. She was quite fearless when it came to trying out new things.

Her father loved her very much and let her do as she wished. Perhaps this was because she had lost her mother when she was only two years old and had no one to teach her all the things that girls of that time had to know. Instead, little Manu grew up insisting on learning to do everything that boys and men did.

'Manu, this is not how girls behave,' Moropant would reason with her when she wanted to try something that was dangerous.

Oh Really?
Moropant Tambe worked as an adviser to the Peshwa's younger brother. He had a salary of Rs 50 a month. Imagine that!

'But, Baba,' she would argue, 'if a boy can do it, why can't I?'

4

Poor Moropant would have no answer to this and would give in, allowing her to do exactly as she pleased.

In those days, it was not common for girls to go to school and study. But not only did Manu learn to read and write in Sanskrit—for she loved reading—she also learnt a little bit of Persian. This made her a very confident young girl and she was never afraid of expressing her views to people. Even though she was not quite eight years old, she was very independent and would insist on doing everything herself.

The Adventurous Threesome

Soon after the death of Manu's mother, Moropant had moved from Kashi to a town called Bithur.

The Peshwas had a large following in Bithur and were the leaders of the Maharashtrian community, playing the role of prime minister as well as the chief of the army.

The boy who was chosen to be the then Peshwa's successor was called Nana Sahib. Nana Sahib was more than ten years older than Manu, but she became great friends with him. From Nana Sahib she learnt horse riding, fencing and even a sport called *mallakhamb*. Tantia Tope was another young man who was Manu's buddy, though he too was much older than her. The three of them became a familiar sight around town, getting up to all sorts of adventurous antics together.

As Manu grew older, she became a skilful horse rider. She also learnt to use weapons. She didn't know it at the time but, later in her life, these skills would become very useful to her.

THE PESHWA AND MANU

Peshwa Baji Rao II would see little Manu running around and making friends with everyone. Wherever Manu went, she would make people smile. The old Peshwa was so fond of her that he nicknamed her Chhabeeli, meaning playful.

Once when Nana Sahib was riding an elephant, Manu insisted on riding one too. When her father forbade her, she sulked and threw a tantrum. She swore that some day she would ride ten elephants!

2 A Whole New World

While young Manu was happily running around and enjoying her unconventional childhood, some events were unfolding that were going to change her life forever. Miles away, in a kingdom called Jhansi, a king of Maharashtrian origin, called Gangadhar Rao, was busy trying to get his kingdom in order. The kings who had ruled before him had mishandled state affairs by wasting money, getting into debt and letting lawless bandits roam free and harass people.

A Wife for the King

Gangadhar Rao, a wise and responsible man, successfully set things straight. The kingdom of Jhansi soon became peaceful and prosperous. His people loved him. But life had a tragedy in store for him. His wife Ramabai died. They had no children and Gangadhar Rao was too busy with matters of the state to think about marrying again.

His advisers and counsellors decided to speak to him.

'Raja Sahib, you must have an heir who will succeed you,' they pleaded.

'But how will I find a woman who has all the qualities of a queen in our community?'

Gangadhar Rao replied absently, his mind preoccupied with official matters.

'Leave that to us,' his advisers said. And they went off in search of the perfect bride for Gangadhar Rao.

A Maharashtrian King in the North?

Jhansi was in the middle of Bundelkhand, a northern region that was ruled by the Rajputs. The Peshwas, on the other hand, were ruling Maharashtra, in the west of India. It so happened that Peshwa Baji Rao I helped a Rajput king called Maharaja Chhatrasal in his battle against Mughal emperor Aurangzeb. Maharaja Chhatrasal was so grateful that, as a reward, he gave Peshwa Baji Rao I a part of his kingdom. Jhansi lay in that region. That is why even though Jhansi was towards the north of India, it was ruled by a Maharashtrian king.

In Bithur, Moropant Tambe was getting anxious about Manu's future.

'How am I ever going to find a nice boy for Manu to marry?' he would say to his friend. 'She can't cook or sew or do any household chores. All she can do is ride horses and play in the streets!'

In those days, girls were married off very young. They were taught to cook, run a household and sew beautifully. All that was required of them was that they look after their husband, their children and their elders. Manu neither had these skills, nor was she brought up in accordance with these traditional beliefs.

Destined to Be Queen

Destiny took a hand in her affairs.

Gangadhar Rao's ministers had heard that there was a large Maharashtrian community in Bithur. They arrived there in the hope of finding a bride for their king.

One day, while discussing their requirements with Moropant, they saw Manu. She was pretty, smart and confident—the perfect qualities for a queen. Moreover, they were struck by her spirit.

Moropant was astounded when the proposal was brought to him. His little Manu, a queen?

'She's too young. She doesn't know the ways of royalty,' he objected half-heartedly. This match was beyond what he had ever hoped for, but he wasn't sure if Manu was up for so much responsibility.

'Oh, don't you worry. We will teach her all there is to know,' Gangadhar Rao's envoys assured Moropant.

When Manu heard about the offer, she protested loud and clear.

'I don't want to leave you, Baba!' she argued.

'Manu, this will be good for your future.

And Gangadhar Rao is a fine and wise king,' Moropant explained patiently. Finally, Manu relented.

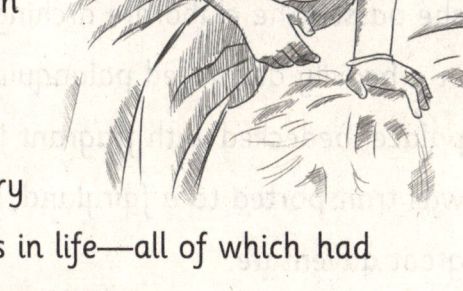

Suddenly, a girl who had only known horses, elephants and rough boyish games had to think about clothes and jewellery and the finer things in life—all of which had never held any interest for her.

A Grand Wedding

A splendid engagement ceremony was held in Bithur. Manu was dressed up in clothes fit for a queen.

'I hate these clothes!' she complained. She wriggled uncomfortably for she was not used to wearing silk saris. But it was something she had to get used to.

If the engagement was grand, the wedding in Jhansi was even grander. Right from the moment she passed the elaborate arching gates of Jhansi in a heavily decorated palanquin to reach the palace, bedecked with fragrant flowers, Manu was transported to a fairyland. It was all a great adventure.

Finally, she saw her future husband.

'He is so old!' was the first thought that came to her mind. She was taken aback for a moment. But she saw that his face was kind and gentle. She felt comforted. She remembered being told that he was a skilled horseman and that made him completely acceptable to her.

There in the midst of such grandeur and ceremony—with the entire city participating in the celebration—at the tender age of fifteen, young Manu became Lakshmibai, the queen of Jhansi.

It's True!

In those days—and even now—in many communities in India, a girl's name is changed after she gets married and she is given a completely new identity.

3 Becoming Queen

Lakshmibai's first few years of being queen proved to be an enormous learning experience.

'Why can't I go outside and ride?' she demanded of her new husband.

'Because that is not what queens do,' Gangadhar Rao explained. 'You must stay indoors and remain behind the purdah when we have visitors.'

'I will not!' Lakshmibai said defiantly. But then she saw the concern in her husband's eyes and relented.

'Okay, I will do as you say, but let me at least ride and get some exercise,' she pleaded.

Gangadhar Rao gave in. He understood her frustration. He made sure she could vent her energy by fencing and riding. Her desire to ride an elephant was still only a dream, but now at least she could take part in some of the sporting activities she was used to.

Did You Know?
It was a custom in many Muslim and Hindu kingdoms that the royal ladies never showed their face to strangers. They stayed behind a curtain called the purdah.

Happily Married

Lakshmibai and Gangadhar Rao soon began to understand each other. She respected him for his wisdom and sense of fairness, while he was amused by his young bride and indulged her.

She even made friends with three young girls—
Sundar, Mandar and Kashi. They were her
maids-in-waiting, who were meant to serve her,
but became her constant companions in all her
adventures.

'You will learn to ride,' she told them.

They were aghast. No girl in Jhansi had ever
been seen riding. They
tried to protest, but
Lakshmibai was much
too persuasive. Soon,
they too became

It's True!
All three girls became so
good at riding that they
fought in battles alongside
Lakshmibai in later years.

proficient riders and began to enjoy the sport as much as their queen did.

Her Own Point of View

Lakshmibai's interests didn't end with sport. She was interested in the affairs of the state too.

'Sitting in this great palace, how will we know whether the people are happy or not?' she demanded of Gangadhar Rao one day. 'I want to ride into the city and meet the poorest of people.'

As always, she was too strong and persuasive, and Gangadhar Rao agreed. Soon she began to make short trips into the city to meet the common people. It reminded her of her childhood days, when she'd run around and play without a care in the world.

She would listen with great interest when her husband discussed important things with his ministers, and she would almost always have a point of view.

Gangadhar was a just but stern man. Sometimes he would be harsh with those who disobeyed him. But Lakshmibai, who had a soft heart, would reason with him.

'That misdeed is not so bad after all,' she would argue if he imposed a particularly harsh punishment on someone. And she would persuade him to give the accused a milder penalty. Soon the people around her began to realize that she was no ordinary queen.

One day, Gangadhar came to Lakshmibai with a suggestion.

'I want you to take charge of the library,' he told her.

Lakshmibai's eyes lit up. She loved reading. She enthusiastically took up the job. Soon she was eagerly reading all the books in the library.

Taking on More Duties

Gradually, Lakshmibai began to take on many more official responsibilities. It was something she enjoyed. And Gangadhar Rao was increasingly happy to leave things to her. He loved music and art and began to devote more time to those pursuits. He listened to court performances for hours, while Lakshmibai found them terribly boring.

Instead she would prefer to ride out of the palace grounds, sometimes in a grand palanquin that her husband had gifted her. Out on the streets, she would interact with all kinds of people.

Life was good. Gangadhar Rao, a generous man, had even made sure that Lakshmibai's father moved to Jhansi, where he gave Moropant a house and an allowance, so that he could be near his beloved daughter.

4 Tragedy Strikes

But sadly, this perfect life was about to change.

After almost nine years of being married, Lakshmibai gave birth to a son. All of Jhansi rejoiced. This was what they had been waiting for—a young prince to take forward his father's dynasty. The baby was named Damodar Rao.

Tragically, however, when he was just a few months old, the baby died. Gangadhar Rao was devastated, as was Lakshmibai. It seemed as though a huge grey cloud had descended on the land of Jhansi. The people couldn't believe this terrible news.

Seriously Ill

Gangadhar Rao was affected the most. He lost interest in everything—his state, the affairs of the people, even the music and arts he loved so much. He became listless. He refused to eat or drink.

'You must be strong for the sake of our people.' Lakshmibai tried to cheer him up in vain. She too was filled with grief but was only too aware of her responsibilities.

Slowly, Gangadhar Rao became weaker and weaker. He took seriously ill.

Around the same time, another problem reared its ugly head. The British, in their arbitrary way, had passed a law that if a king died without an heir, their kingdom would automatically come under British rule. This hateful law was called the

Doctrine of Lapse.
It was the brainchild of
Lord Dalhousie, who was
the governor general
of India at that time.

UNFAIR LAWS

The British had long wanted to extend their empire to India. They knew India was wealthy and had a rich history. They began by trading with India in the 1600s. They set up a company called the East India Company. But slowly, they sent soldiers and began to battle with the ruling kings. One by one, they defeated the kings, took over entire regions and soon were ruling all over India, which had become a British colony. By the year 1858, India was known as British India. And they passed many laws that were unfair to Indians. The Doctrine of Lapse was just one of them.

In spite of being so ill, Gangadhar Rao was aware of and worried about the Doctrine of Lapse. He thought the only solution was to adopt a son, which would prevent his kingdom from being annexed and, at the same time, give him the heir he so longed for. One of his close relatives had a son who was about five years old. Gangadhar Rao decided to adopt him immediately.

His ministers drew up all the legal papers, and Gangadhar Rao and Lakshmibai adopted the little boy as their own son. He was renamed Damodar Rao in memory of their lost baby.

'You will be my own boy,' Lakshmibai said, hugging little Damodar. She promised to give him all the love and attention she would have given her own baby.

Keeping in mind the random decisions that the British were known to take, Gangadhar Rao wanted to make sure that young Damodar was accepted as his heir even by the British.

He wrote an official letter to Lord Dalhousie informing him of what he had done. He also gave up his position as king, in the presence of two British officers, Major Ellis and Captain Martin, so that Damodar Rao could be proclaimed king before his own death.

The King Is No More

But Gangadhar Rao's health kept deteriorating. His fever intensified and he became gravely ill. He could hardly sit up. Lakshmibai was by his side day and night. Major Ellis, who was a sympathizer of Gangadhar Rao and Lakshmibai, even brought a British doctor to treat him. But nothing worked. And one dark day, Gangadhar Rao gave up the fight and died.

Lakshmibai was inconsolable. She was barely twenty-six and already a widow. She had truly loved her husband, even though he was so much older than her.

For once in her life, she did exactly what tradition demanded. She stopped wearing the magnificent jewellery and colourful silk saris befitting a queen. Instead she wore only white clothes, as was the custom at the time. But she refused to shave her head or hide behind the purdah.

She prayed all day long for her country and for peace. She maintained strict discipline and stayed in mourning for a long time. All of Jhansi was cast in gloom. The people were worried. Countrywide, there were dreadful stories of how the British were taking over regions that didn't have a king.

Finally, Lakshmibai—ever responsible and conscious of her duties as queen—realized she needed to shake herself out of her grief. 'There is much to be done,' she thought. So she put the past behind her, drew a deep breath and prepared to face what the future was to bring.

> ### Did You Know?
> In those days, it was a custom among some communities for women to shave their heads when their husbands died. People say this was done to make sure that these women never married again and that they were recognized as widows. It was a cruel ritual.

5 A Nasty Turn of Fate

Once more, fate was playing its own games with Lakshmibai. The letter that Gangadhar Rao had written to Lord Dalhousie, requesting him to accept Damodar Rao as his official heir, took nearly five months to reach the governor general.

A British agent called Malcolm, who did a lot of work for the East India Company, did not want Lord Dalhousie to accept Damodar Rao as king. So he wrote a letter in which he reminded Lord Dalhousie that even if a king wanted to adopt an heir, he had to take the East India Company's permission first and that Gangadhar Rao had not done so.

Unjust Advice

Not just that, Malcolm took matters into his own hands. He suggested that Lakshmibai was only a woman and that Damodar Rao was too young. So Jhansi would be better off if the British ruled over it.

'Ask the queen to leave the fort in which she lives,' Malcolm advised Lord Dalhousie in his letter. 'Jhansi must now belong to the British and the British only. We must not recognize either Lakshmibai or her adopted son, Damodar Rao.'

Of course, Lakshmibai had no idea about all this. She was busy making arrangements to crown her young prince the king. She had also gone back to something she loved—managing the affairs of Jhansi.

A Disciplined Routine

Life took on a new routine. Lakshmibai continued to exercise as well as pray. She groomed young Damodar in the ways of royalty, determined to make him a strong prince and, eventually, a great king. She met her ministers to discuss the issues of the people. Slowly, Jhansi, which had been under a cloud of grief, began to shine brightly again. She truly was on her way to becoming a great queen.

But Lakshmibai was a practical woman. She knew that without the support of the British, everything could be snatched away in an instant. When no

reply came from Lord Dalhousie for many months, she wrote to him with a reminder even as she continued her work.

A New Problem

In the meantime, she had another problem to face. A man called Sadashiv Rao Newalkar, who was a distant nephew of her husband, Gangadhar Rao, suddenly appeared.

'I am a direct descendant of Gangadhar's family,' he claimed. 'I am the rightful heir to the throne of Jhansi.'

There was confusion all around. But Lakshmibai was not in the least perturbed. She felt confident that the British would support her and accept Damodar as the official heir.

A Rude Shock

Imagine her shock when Major Ellis arrived with a letter that shook her entire world.

The whole court had gathered. Lakshmibai sat behind a curtain, for she refused to show herself to the British, though she didn't stay behind the purdah at other times. Major Ellis had Lord Dalhousie's order in his hand. He read it out:

> From this day on, Jhansi will be under the British. We do not recognize Damodar Rao as the legal heir.

There was a stunned silence.

Then suddenly, Lakshmibai cried out loud and clear, 'I will *never* give up my Jhansi!'

She rose and furiously stormed out of the court. This was a totally unfair decision, she felt.

The British demanded that she leave the fort that had been her home for so many years. But they decided to allow her to live in her palace and to give her Rs 5000 every month for her expenses. But she would no longer be queen. For Lakshmibai, it was the end of life as she knew it. Suddenly, her home, her land, her people were no longer hers. It seemed as though she would have to start her life all over again.

Oh Really?

When Damodar was born, though he was nowhere in line to become a king, astrologers looked at his stars and prophesized that he was destined to rule. And as fate would have it, he was adopted by the king of Jhansi and led a royal life for a while.

6 More Troubles

Once again, Lakshmibai chose to be practical. Rather than make a fuss, she opted to go with the decision of the British—at least for the time being.

'Come on, let's pack up,' she told her staff.

Many people worked for the royal family. Attendants, cooks, grooms who looked after the horses and elephants, bodyguards, soldiers and, of course, all her ministers. They were all devastated at having to leave the fort in which they had spent so many happy years in the service of this kind

and generous queen. But, like Lakshmibai, they too had no choice.

Being Smart

Although Lakshmibai had accepted the Company's decision, she was playing it smart.

> **Did You Know?**
> Rani Lakshmibai had three favourite horses. They were called Sarangi, Pavan and Badal.

Over the years, she had built up a lot of military weaponry. And she had no intention of leaving it all behind so that the treacherous British could use it. Under her orders, some of the largest cannons were buried deep underground. She decided to take a lot of other arms along with her.

There was a secret passage that led from the fort to the palace in which she would now live. She ordered that the passage be blocked.

And finally, amid tears and lamentation from her people, the queen left her fort and went to live in the much smaller palace with her staff.

Now she had to go back to her early life as a commoner. But not for a moment did she forget either her position or her responsibility to her people.

'We will convince the British that what they have done is wrong,' she thought. She persistently wrote letters and petitions—first to Lord Dalhousie, and then directly to England. But none were answered.

The queen turned her attention to her son. 'I will prepare Damodar for his destiny,' she decided. 'One day, he will surely rule.'

She had Damodar learn Persian and Sanskrit. She taught him to ride and build his stamina and strength, all the while making sure that she too remained in top form. This discipline was of great use later.

Taking Away What Was Hers

It was bad enough that the British had taken away Lakshmibai's throne and fort. Now they were about to heap more insults and troubles upon the brave queen.

Lakshmibai's husband, Gangadhar, had inherited an empire ridden with debts to the British Raj. He had managed to repay most of it. But there was still a certain sum that was owed by the time he died. The British now decided to deduct that amount from the allowance they gave the queen every month.

The injustice did not stop there. Even though the British did not accept Damodar Rao as the heir to the Jhansi throne, he was still entitled to a lot of money, jewellery and the houses that belonged to his adopted father, Gangadhar Rao. Instead of handing all this over to the boy's guardian, Lakshmibai, the British decided to lock it up till Damodar Rao became an adult.

Making Ends Meet

Both these actions deprived Lakshmibai of what was rightfully hers and placed her in a difficult situation. She, a queen who once lived in luxury, now had to learn to manage with far less.

Never one to give up, Lakshmibai held her head high. She was frugal and managed her household with what little she had. She continued her routine of exercise. And this time, she was joined not only by her close friends, but by many more women who wished to break free from tradition. And thus was born a secret army of women, who went on to play an important role in Lakshmibai's life in the near future.

7 India Rebels

While Lakshmibai was facing her own problems, more trouble was brewing across the country. The British, who had entered India as a trading company, had now begun to take the law into their own hands.

Anger Builds

The British put in place many laws that were indescribably cruel and unfair. They imposed heavy taxes on the poorest farmers and meted out heavier punishment if they were unable to pay. They abruptly stopped worship at temples, even destroying some of them. They set up slaughterhouses, where pigs and cows were butchered for their meat, right in the middle of cities. Both Muslims and Hindus were deeply offended by this act. And when anyone protested, they were immediately jailed.

The final straw came when it was rumoured that the cartridges given to the Indian soldiers in the British Army were coated with animal fat. This infuriated the soldiers, most of whom were deeply religious. Using particular meats was against their religion, and they needed to bite the cartridges before using them.

A Fierce Rebellion

There was a fierce rebellion. Soldiers marched to Delhi, asking the Mughal emperor Bahadur Shah Zafar to take over the reins. British officers who got in the way were killed. More and more civilians joined the rebellion. And soon, the whole of India was in the grip of protests that were turning violent.

Lakshmibai watched this with concern. On the one hand, she too wanted the British to go away.

On the other, she hated violence of any kind.
Meanwhile, the rioting was coming closer to
home—to Jhansi. The British living in and around
Jhansi started to get worried.

Protecting the Innocent

The rebelling Indian sepoys marched towards
Jhansi. They knew that Jhansi was in a
strategically important location for the British
and that gaining control of the city would weaken
them. At their end, the British armies saw the

approaching trouble. They decided to send their families to Jhansi Fort, where they believed they would be safe.

But Lakshmibai feared the wrath of the crowds. There were only a few soldiers left who were loyal to the British and would protect the innocent women and children at Jhansi Fort.

'Send the women and children to my palace,' she told the British commanding officer. 'I have fewer guards but they will do as I tell them. I will be better able to protect your families.'

Even though the British had been so nasty to her, Lakshmibai could not bear their families getting hurt.

Lakshmibai had a soft heart beneath her tough exterior. She felt for the British women and children—and even the British soldiers, who were in such great danger at Jhansi Fort. Knowing that there was limited food in the fort, Lakshmibai ordered for the passage between the fort and her palace to be opened up. She instructed her cooks to make hundreds of rotis and sent them to the fort with her three trusted maids.

A Bloodbath

The commanding officer, however, paid no heed. He thought he could get the rebel soldiers under control. But the worst happened. The furious Indian sepoys mercilessly killed most of the British who were taking shelter at Jhansi Fort.

Lakshmibai was horrified. Worse was to follow. Crowds of Indian soldiers yelled slogans outside her palace.

'We will give you back the Jhansi throne!' they shouted. 'But you have to give us money so we can feed our rebels and continue our fight!'

Lakshmibai didn't know what to do. She didn't have so much money. But if she didn't give them something, she feared that, in their mad fury, they might harm civilians. It was a delicate situation and she had to act carefully.

She addressed the rebelling soldiers from the window of her palace. 'You know that the British have taken away all my money and everything I own,' she called out boldly. 'I will give you the only precious thing I have left. Here is my diamond necklace.'

She threw down her diamond necklace, which in those days was worth the princely sum of more than Rs 1 lakh. Satisfied, the shouting crowd went away.

Lakshmibai breathed a sigh of relief. She returned to taking care of other pressing matters.

In the following days, the British became busy handling the riots and uprisings all over the country, and they temporarily returned the reins of Jhansi to the queen.

That's Amazing!
In those days, Rs 1 lakh could feed an entire village for a year or more!

For a while at least, Lakshmibai was the queen of Jhansi once again.

8 Greater Challenges in Store

You would think that now that Lakshmibai was back on the throne, things would be peaceful. And they were—for a very short while.

Knowing that the British could change their mind at any moment, Lakshmibai decided that she must get ready.

'If the British attack, I should be prepared,' she thought. 'I will not give in this time, no matter what happens.'

Gearing Up

She began to rebuild her army. When the British had ousted her, her massive army had been broken apart. She gathered as many of her former troops as possible. They came from diverse communities, but all of them were deeply loyal to her.

The queen began to train them rigorously, making sure they were battle ready at all times.

Not only that, she equipped them with enough weaponry. She dug out the cannons she had buried when she left the fort and made sure they were in top condition.

Lakshmibai stopped wearing her traditional attire and began to dress like a soldier when she rode. She wore trousers, a jacket and a turban. It was only at home that she donned the white sari that widows wore.

Trouble Erupts

Sadly for Lakshmibai, fresh, unexpected trouble was just around the corner. Sadashiv Rao Newalkar showed up once again.

'I am the rightful heir to the kingdom of Jhansi,' he proclaimed imperiously. Now that the British were out of the way, he wanted the throne for himself.

He gathered an army of 3000 soldiers and launched an attack on the regions surrounding Jhansi. He told all and sundry that he was the king of Jhansi, and took to plundering the neighbouring areas and harassing the people.

Lakshmibai didn't waste a moment. She rounded up her troops and went to war against Sadashiv Rao. She easily overcame his army and imprisoned him deep in the dungeons of Jhansi Fort.

That was one obstacle removed. But more was in store for Lakshmibai.

Betrayed by Her Neighbours

Historically, the northern part of India, where Jhansi is located, was ruled by Rajput kings. Jhansi was an exception, where the Marathas ruled. For many years, the Rajput kings accepted this and, in fact, were on good terms with the rulers of Jhansi in the past.

But now, two Rajput kingdoms began to object to the idea that there was a Maratha kingdom in the middle of a Rajput stronghold.

The kings of the Rajput states Orchha and Datia joined forces to attack Jhansi. They decided that they would defeat Lakshmibai and divide the wealth and kingdom of Jhansi between themselves.

A queen called Ladaiya Rani, who ruled the kingdom of Orchha, took the lead. Her army, along with Datia's army, mounted a fierce attack on Jhansi.

But Lakshmibai was fully prepared. Her army
was in prime condition. Her ammunition and
weaponry was newly spruced up. She was in peak
form. She commandeered her troops and led them
into battle.

A terrible war raged for more than twenty days.
Lakshmibai fought from the front the whole time.
Many soldiers were wounded and killed on both
sides. But in the end, it was Lakshmibai's army
that won the battle. The armies of Orchha and
Datia were forced to withdraw.

It's True!

Lakshmibai had a powerful cannon that was nicknamed Kadak Bijli (meaning blinding lightning). The cannon's mouth was in the shape of a lion and it could shoot missiles up to a great distance. This cannon was one of the reasons that Lakshmibai's artillery was so effective.

There was joyous celebration in Jhansi. It seemed as if the people of Jhansi loved their queen more than ever before. For some time, peace prevailed.

A Wise and Good Queen

Lakshmibai spent her days fortifying her kingdom. She was not quite thirty years of age but already wiser than her years.

She made sure she listened to the troubles of every subject—however insignificant. There are many stories of her compassion for the poor: how she had warm clothes made for them during winter;

how she regularly distributed food to those who needed it; how she listened to any person who wished to talk to her.

Still training rigorously, she started practising shooting while riding—it is said—by holding the reins of the horse in her teeth. It's no wonder she became one of the most skilled riders in India.

The Schedule of a Queen

Lakshmibai never strayed from her routine, unless she was at war.

- She would wake up every morning as early as 4 a.m.
- Then she would pray, bathe and meditate.
- Next, she would go horse riding, and practise shooting and swordsmanship.
- She made sure to spend time with her dear son, Damodar, who was growing up fast.

- She would then bathe again, before she went out to feed the poor and the hungry.
- After a brief rest, she would read the Ramayana or the Bhagavad Gita.
- Then she would meet her ministers to see to matters of the state.
- After another round of prayer and meditation, her day would end.

What amazing discipline!

9 A Battle Rages

All through this time, though Jhansi had a short period of peace, the rest of India was in the throes of protest. The British were constantly quelling rebellions. Even civilians had taken to rioting on the streets.

In the meantime, the leaders of the East India Company were keeping an eye on Jhansi.

'This woman is getting too strong,' they thought. 'She has easily defeated the rulers of Orchha and Datia. How long will it be before she challenges us?'

Stop the Rani

Their spies had kept them informed of how she also vanquished and imprisoned Sadashiv Rao, the man who had tried to claim the throne of Jhansi. The British were aware that she was building a strong army and also stocking up on weapons, gunpowder and other ammunition.

They decided that she should be stopped before she became too big a force for them to handle.

By this time, British India had a new governor general named Lord Canning. After Lord Dalhousie, it was now his turn to try to overpower Lakshmibai.

Having learnt from Lord Dalhousie exactly how strong and focused Lakshmibai was, Lord Canning decided to play very safe.

A New British Commander

'We cannot underestimate this woman,' Lord Canning told his lieutenants. 'I want our most experienced soldier to lead a campaign against Jhansi.' He chose a man called Sir Hugh Rose to lead this battle.

Sir Hugh Rose had a lot of experience in warfare. He had fought many battles in his lifetime and knew all about war strategies. His army was made up of specially trained British soldiers and the best and most loyal Indian sepoys. Not just that, he was supported by an army of the

Oh Really?
Many years later, when Sir Hugh Rose wrote about his life in India, he said how impressed he had been with Rani Lakshmibai. He called her 'clever and beautiful'.

Nizam of Hyderabad. The rulers of Orchha and Datia also helped the British with their own troops and ammunition.

Marching to Jhansi

One early spring morning, Sir Hugh's troops began the long march to Jhansi from Mhow, the town where the army was gathered. There were many sepoys who had broken away from the British Army and joined forces with their Indian brothers. It wasn't a simple march. There were several obstacles that they had to overcome along the way.

Did You Know?
The word sepoy comes from the Hindi word *sipahi*, meaning soldier.

Oh Really?
Rao Sahib, Rani Lakshmibai's childhood friend, tried to attack Sir Hugh's army and stop him. Sadly, he wasn't up to the task. He and his army retreated hurriedly when they were met with a strong counter-attack by the British.

Some sepoys rebelled and slowed down the British Army's progress. Some Indian kings and rebel leaders decided to attack Sir Hugh's troops while they were on the way to Jhansi. This hindered the troops, but did not stop Sir Hugh.

Lakshmibai's spies came to report the events to her. They had been given the task of keeping a sharp eye on all British activities and reporting them at once to the queen.

'Rani Sahiba,' they said, 'a man called Sir Hugh Rose is on his way to Jhansi with a big regiment of soldiers. They want to capture Jhansi and throw you out.'

'Is that so?' Lakshmibai's eyes flashed with fury. 'Well, let them come. We will show them what we are made of!'

She got into action at once. Her first step was to do something to slow down Sir Hugh's progress.

She sent her people to scorch the land so that there would be no fodder for Sir Hugh's horses. She then ordered that all the crops and vegetables in the farms surrounding Jhansi be cut and sent to Jhansi for safekeeping—thus stopping the flow of food to Sir Hugh's troops. She wanted to avoid war at any cost, for she knew that war simply brought about death and destruction.

At the same time, she stayed completely prepared.

Ready for Battle

'Keep our cannons ready. Load the gunpowder. And be prepared to fight,' she ordered her troops.

Her army was on high alert. She stocked the fort with enough food for all the people living there, for she realized they might have to be holed up in the fort for weeks or more in case of war.

'Damodar,' she said, taking her son aside one evening, 'we are preparing for battle. You must

make sure that even if I am busy, you continue with your studies, your riding and sword fighting.'

Damodar nodded seriously. He loved his mother and wanted to make her proud. For her part, she wanted him to have all the skills a king would need, for she intended to make sure he reigned one day.

Eventually, Sir Hugh and his troops made their way into Jhansi. They had been slowed down but had refused to stop.

No matter—Lakshmibai was ready.

Lakshmibai was not alone; she had a lot of supporters. Her childhood friend Tantia Tope stood by her side, ready to go to war. He promised his army of 25,000 soldiers to add strength. Rao Sahib, the rani's long-time friend, resolved to help this time as well and also joined her. Both of them had been harassed by the British and were more than willing to fight them.

That's Amazing!

Lakshmibai devised a system of information that kept her aware of the enemy's progress. Every village was alerted. A method was put in place by which if even a single British soldier was spotted, a fire was lit on a hillock. As soon as the next village spotted the signal, they too would do the same. And in this manner, village after village would be alerted and the news would eventually reach Rani Lakshmibai.

Finally, Sir Hugh, along with his massive army, reached the outskirts of Jhansi. The battle was about to begin.

Did You Know?

Tantia Tope is believed to have fought over 150 battles with the British and defeated more than 10,000 British soldiers.

10 A Fierce Combat

There are different versions of what happened next. Some say that Sir Hugh first tried to have talks with Lakshmibai to convince her to give up Jhansi without a fight. Yet others say he had his armies ride up in stealth to take her by surprise.

In either case, a fierce battle took place. Sir Hugh really was a clever battle strategist. He had studied the fort carefully, and he wanted his army to break down the weakest wall of the fort so they could enter it and capture Lakshmibai.

But he had not taken into account the full strength and weaponry of Lakshmibai's army.

Battle Cry

'Har har Mahadev!' shouted Lakshmibai.

This was the Maratha war cry. Her soldiers sprang into action. Cannons exploded. There was furious gunfire. Lakshmibai herself went from gunner to gunner, encouraging, advising and strategizing. The women of her army fought side by side with the men.

They had to refill the guns and cannons as soon as they were fired. Kadak Bijli was doing its job brilliantly. It was accompanied by another cannon, which the locals called Ghanagarj (meaning thunder). Thus, the army of Jhansi rained thunder and lightning on the British troops.

Oh Really?

Lakshmibai had trained many women to fight like her. In fact, she had an army of women known as the Durga Dal, which valiantly fought alongside her in battle.

The British were taken aback. They did not expect this level of readiness or skill. Many of their soldiers died. There was a brief respite when the British stepped back to formulate a new strategy. They soon came back with renewed vigour.

A Furious Attack

This time, their attack was even more ferocious. They incessantly fired cartridges and balls of fire into the fort. One after another, Lakshmibai lost her most trusted warriors. Lalubhau Bakshi, Ghulam Ghaus Khan, Khuda Baksh, Kashi Bai and Moti Bai—all these were brave men and women who had fought with all their heart by Rani Lakshmibai's side. As each bold warrior fell, Lakshmibai felt as though a knife were being driven into her heart. But she would pick herself up and move on with the fight.

Tantia's Support

The British gunners had now reached the homes of the villagers. Houses were set on fire and people were forced to flee from their homes. Sir Hugh's men shot and burst the main water reservoir from where the fort received drinking water. Now water and food were running low too.

Just as Lakshmibai and her army were reaching breaking point, there was a cry of triumph.

'Tantia Tope's army has arrived!' someone shouted.

There was a cheer and sighs of relief. The British were diverted. Tantia Tope's army of more than 20,000 soldiers had attacked Sir Hugh's army from outside the periphery of the town. They fought the British fiercely. But perhaps because a section of his troops were raw recruits and could not face the ferocity of the battle, the British overcame Tantia Tope's regiment too.

The Fort Is Captured

Lakshmibai was stretched to capacity. She had not slept or eaten for days and was like a woman possessed.

Finally, the British broke down one wall of the fort. They entered it, looting the treasures and setting fire to everything else they saw. They burnt the temples, broke down doors and windows, set fire to Lakshmibai's beloved library and ripped the precious stones from the furniture and the walls. They ruthlessly killed women and children, cutting down anyone and anything that came in their way.

Now Lakshmibai had no more defences. She gathered her remaining captains.

'There is no help for it. We will surely get captured by the British. And I refuse to be their prisoner,' she said. 'I would rather set myself on fire than spend a day in captivity.'

'No, Rani Sahiba!' said one of her senior advisers.
'You must think of Damodar. And you must
get away safely, and one day we can still
reclaim Jhansi.'

Escape

Lakshmibai looked at him for a long moment. She
now knew what she had to do. She had to keep
herself and her son, Damodar, safe so that she
could win Jhansi back sometime in the future.

Without wasting another moment, she saddled
her beloved horse Sarangi and, strapping young
Damodar to her back, escaped from the fort.

Oh Really?

Legend says that Lakshmibai leapt from the high walls of the fort when she escaped the British. No one knows if this is true, because the walls of the fort are so high that it would be almost impossible to leap from there without losing one's life. But it's a legend that mothers love to recount to their children to this day.

Did You Know?

Jhalkari Bai was one of Lakshmibai's most trusted soldiers from her women's army. She was known to be so brave and strong that, according to a story, she single-handedly killed a tiger that attacked her!

11 The Final Fight

Lakshmibai rode through the city like the wind. Her dear friend Jhalkari disguised herself as the queen to fool the British and rode out in a different direction. For a long time, British soldiers followed Jhalkari, thinking she was indeed Rani Lakshmibai. When they discovered that they had been fooled, a massive hunt for Lakshmibai was organized.

Lakshmibai managed to find her way to a town called Kalpi, where her unsuccessful ally Rao Sahib had set up camp. With Damodar, she rode into the camp exhausted.

She was welcomed and immediately made to rest. Some of her friends, like Tantia Tope, were already there, while others were arriving with their troops.

Preparing to Fight Back

'We must fight the British,' they said when they all got together to decide what they needed to do next. Lakshmibai gave her opinion on how she felt they should proceed.

'We must train our troops to withstand the British,' she said. 'I know how the British think. And how strong their army is. We must be even better prepared.'

She trained her troops from morning to night, never feeling tired herself. But when it was time for the battle, to her shock and dismay, Rao Sahib decided it was he and not Lakshmibai who would lead the troops.

It was a mistake that cost them.

Meanwhile, Sir Hugh had discovered that Rani Lakshmibai was in Kalpi. He decided to attack. Under the cover of night, he arrived in town. But neither Tantia Tope nor Rao Sahib was up for the fight. However, Lakshmibai fought long and hard, alongside the soldiers.

A Battle Lost

But the strategy that Rao Sahib had employed did not work at all. The battle wasn't a long one.

Even though the British soldiers were exhausted by the May heat, they easily overcame the rebel troops.

Many lives were lost, and Rao Sahib's army had to accept defeat. But Lakshmibai, Tantia Tope and Rao Sahib himself managed to escape once again. Lakshmibai, for once in her life, felt helpless.

That night, Rao Sahib went to Lakshmibai's tent.

'It was my mistake,' he admitted sheepishly. 'I beg you to take over and lead our troops from now on.'

Lakshmibai agreed. She was focused on only one thing—to fight for her country and drive the British away.

Heading to Gwalior

A new opportunity came her way. Gwalior was a rich state. And the Scindias, the rulers of Gwalior, were supporters of the British.

'We must capture Gwalior,' Lakshmibai decided. 'This will be the next step in our revolt. It will send a message to the British.'

Without delay, she commandeered her troops and marched into battle. When the Scindia soldiers, who were supporting the British Army, realized that the enemy charge was being led by the rani of Jhansi, they suddenly changed sides and went from fighting *against* Lakshmibai to fighting in

her army. And so Lakshmibai and her army easily captured Gwalior.

A Minor Victory

Loud cheers broke out among Lakshmibai's troops. Gwalior was certainly a prize. Now all the wealth of the state—the gold coins, the precious stones—belonged to the attacking rebel army.

'We must not be greedy,' Lakshmibai said. 'We will use this wealth to continue our rebellion.'

She made sure that none of Gwalior's treasures, temples or monuments were destroyed. But the wealth was distributed among Tantia Tope, Rao Sahib, her lieutenants and herself.

'Rani Lakshmibai has captured Gwalior!' At another camp, the British spies arrived breathlessly to give the news to Sir Hugh.

'How can this be?' thundered Sir Hugh. 'We cannot allow this! We must overthrow her at once. Get the troops ready,' he ordered.

Once again, the British were ready to chase Lakshmibai. She was really a thorn in their side, and they would not rest until they had dislodged her.

No Time to Rest

'Sir Hugh is on his way to Gwalior,' Lakshmibai's spies reported.

There seemed to be no rest for her. She sighed. Then she called all her supporters and friends.

'My friends, this will be a hard battle,' she told them. 'We must fight for our country no matter what happens.'

It was as if she could see what was to happen. She embraced Damodar tightly.

'Look after him if anything happens to me,' she told Mandar and Kashi, her friends from Jhansi. And, turning, she walked off to organize her troops.

The Last Fight

Lakshmibai dressed in the same clothes as her soldiers, passing off as a man. The battle that followed was terrible. But this time, Lakshmibai's troops were not as well equipped. Whereas the British army was better prepared than ever before.

They attacked from all sides, and soon Lakshmibai was cut off from her troops. Many soldiers were killed on both sides and blood flowed freely on the battleground.

The Queen Falls

Lakshmibai fought furiously. A group of British soldiers cornered the lone warrior, who was slim and short. They didn't know it was a woman, least of all Lakshmibai herself. Suddenly, she felt a sharp blow and a piercing pain. She had been hit. No one is sure if it was a bullet or a sword that delivered the fatal blow. This time, she could not get up. She fell forward on her horse, bleeding.

The British soldiers, thinking her dead, moved on. For many hours, Lakshmibai's beloved horse Sarangi carried her body, trotting aimlessly, looking for help. Finally, one of her loyal men found the horse.

Oh Really?

Lakshmibai did not want her body to fall into the hands of the British. Eventually, some locals cremated her. A monument stands in Gwalior at the spot where she died.

He took the reins and quickly made for the nearest camp to get help for the dying Lakshmibai. But it was too late.

'Har har Mahadev,' were Rani Lakshmibai's last words. Then she finally gave up her life, having fought till her last breath. Her last thoughts were for her country and her son.

Damodar was given a small pension by the British, and he lived like a commoner. He never got his inheritance.

Rani Lakshmibai lived and died like a true queen. Even now, so many years later, people remember her for her bravery, her strength and her patriotism.

She may have been crowned in Jhansi and died in Gwalior, but she still lives in the minds and hearts of over a billion people across India.

Imagine That!

After Rani Lakshmibai was killed, young Damodar Rao, with some loyal soldiers, had to look for shelter. They roamed from place to place. Finally, they reached a village and promised to pay the headman Rs 500 every month, along with nine horses and four camels. And in return, the villagers would give them food and shelter, and also tell them if any British soldiers were around.

Did You Know?

There was a unit in the Indian National Army called the Rani of Jhansi Regiment, which was entirely composed of women. It was led by Captain Lakshmi. Such a coincidence that her name was Lakshmi too!

12 Timeline

ca 1827	Moropant Tambe and Bhagirathi Bai become parents to Manikarnika Tambe in Kashi.
1829	Bhagirathi Bai dies, leaving Manikarnika motherless.
1842	Manikarnika gets married to Gangadhar Rao, ruler of Jhansi, and becomes Lakshmibai, queen of Jhansi.
1851	Lakshmibai gives birth to a baby boy, who dies within a few months.
1853	Gangadhar Rao and Lakshmibai adopt a little boy, whom they rename Damodar Rao.
1853	Gangadhar Rao dies.
1854	Lord Dalhousie takes over Jhansi under the Doctrine of Lapse.
1857	Indian sepoys begin to rebel against the British.
April 1858	Sir Hugh Rose leads a battle against Lakshmibai in Jhansi and defeats her.
May 1858	Rani Lakshmibai, Tantia Tope and Rao Sahib lose the battle against the British in Kalpi.
June 1858	Rani Lakshmibai's army conquers Gwalior.
June 1858	Sir Hugh sends an army to Gwalior, defeating Rani Lakshmibai's troops.
18 June 1858	Rani Lakshmibai is killed in battle.

13 Stories of Other Warrior Queens

Just like Rani Lakshmibai of Jhansi, there have been many warrior queens in India and across the world, who have bravely fought battles and stood up for their rights and their kingdoms. Here's a glimpse into some of their lives, their incredible courage and their fascinating stories.

Razia Sultana (1205-40)

Iltutmish was the ruler of the Delhi Sultanate. Though he had sons, it was his daughter Razia Sultana, who showed signs of being a great leader. She was trained in fighting, riding and administration, for her father had decided that she would be his successor.

But when the time came, her brother cunningly claimed the throne. True to her father's wishes, she fought her brother, overthrew him and became queen. During her successful rule, she built roads and wells and promoted art and culture.

Razia Sultana gave up her feminine attire and was always dressed in the garb of a soldier. The Turkish nobles were not happy being ruled by a woman. They conspired against Razia Sultana and her husband, who was the governor of Bhatinda (now called Bathinda). While Razia was away on a royal visit, her half-brother usurped the throne. She fought valiantly, but she and her husband were both killed.

Razia Sultana has gone down in history as being the first woman to rule over the Delhi Sultanate.

Rani Velu Nachiyar (1730–96)

Rani Velu Nachiyar is believed to be the first woman of Tamil origin to fight the British. The queen of the Tamil kingdom of Sivaganga, Rani Velu, as she was called, was skilled in martial arts, archery, horse riding and the use of weapons. As the only child of her father, it was assumed that she would become queen.

When she turned sixteen, she married Muthuvaduganathur, the king of Sivaganga. The next twenty years passed in great peace. But then the British arrived. They stormed her palace in an attempt to take over her kingdom. Her husband was killed. Rani Velu was infuriated. Putting her grief aside, she picked up arms and led her army against the British.

She formed an all-women's army and put up a brave fight. She discovered where the British had hidden their ammunition and sent a faithful female soldier, as a human bomb, to destroy it all. She won her kingdom back from the British and ruled it until her death.

Rani Rudrama Devi (ca 1259–ca 1289)

Rani Rudrama Devi ruled the Kakatiya Empire when her father died and became the first and only woman to rule Andhra Pradesh. When she became queen, many warlords from her kingdom did not at all like the idea of being ruled by a woman. They plotted against her, but she fought them successfully.

She married a man called Veera Bhadra, but sadly, she was soon widowed. She was devastated, but never forgot her responsibilities as queen. Seeing that the kingdom was ruled by a queen, many kings tried to invade it, thinking it would be easy to overthrow her. They did not account for her bravery and skill. She defeated all the attackers. During her reign, she built the famous Warangal Fort and also captured many forts. Under her leadership, the army was strong and capable. People say she died of an injury she sustained during a battle.

Veera Shiromani Keladi Chennamma (1671–96)

Keladi was a small kingdom in what is now Karnataka. When the king of Keladi died, his wife, Veera Shiromani Keladi Chennamma, took over the throne. She ruled for more than twenty years. She was an able and wise queen, and her kingdom prospered under her.

Keladi Chennamma took up arms when her kingdom was attacked by the fierce and ruthless Mughal emperor Aurangzeb. She rallied her troops and went fearlessly into battle with him. She successfully held off Aurangzeb's army. As a sworn enemy of the Mughals, she sheltered Rajaram, son of Maratha king Chhattrapati Shivaji. In a later battle, she defeated the king of Mysore.

As an able administrator, she signed a treaty with the Portuguese and allowed them to build churches in her kingdom. She was a warrior queen who is perhaps not famous across the world, but is a hero to her people.

Empress Septimia Zenobia (ca 240–Unknown)

Septimia Zenobia was a queen born in the third century. She ruled the Palmyrene Empire (present-day Syria). When her husband, the king Odaenathus, was assassinated, instead of sitting back, she took over the empire on behalf of her young son and declared herself empress. Not content to simply rule, she decided to expand her empire. She invaded and captured many lands, all the way to Egypt.

But the Roman Empire, which was the mightiest empire at that time, still remained out of her reach. She fought battles with the Romans but could not withstand their mighty armies. She was defeated and spent the rest of her days in exile. But her bravery and determination are legendary and even now, the people of Syria regard her as a heroine.

Queen Anna Nzinga (ca 1583–ca 1663)

Anna Nzinga was the brave warrior queen of the kingdoms of Ndongo and Matamba (parts of present-day Angola, in Africa). She is known mostly for the way she fought the Portuguese and kept her kingdom free from colonial rule. The Portuguese had spotted the kingdoms of Ndongo and Matamba, and they began invading these lands with the intention of capturing people and making them slaves. They also knew these regions were rich in silver.

But Anna Nzinga would have none of it. She led her troops into battle and fought fiercely. She successfully kept the Portuguese at bay and, during her rule, was able to transform her kingdom into a force as powerful as the Portuguese.

Lady Trieu Thi Trinh (225–248)

Many years before Trieu Thi Trinh was born, the Chinese Han dynasty had taken control of Vietnam. For hundreds of years, the Chinese ruled Vietnam, imposing their laws and way of life. The Vietnamese people never accepted the Chinese and longed to have their independence. It was at this time that young Trieu Thi Trinh decided to rebel. She was just twenty years old when she began to raise a secret army to fight the Chinese. She built an army of a thousand people and led them into battle. It is said that she carried two swords and fearlessly rode an elephant on to the battlefield.

She liberated her village and the area surrounding it. But such a small army could not withstand the fury of the mighty Chinese Army. Trieu Thi Trinh was defeated, dying when she was just twenty-three years old. But such is her heroism that even today, a national holiday is observed in her honour, and many streets in Vietnam bear her name.

Queen Boudicca (ca 30–ca 61)

Boudicca was the wife of King Prasutagus, the ruler of the Celtic tribe of Iceni. When he died, his will stated that his kingdom be jointly divided between the Roman Empire and his two daughters. But far from honouring his will, the Romans tortured Queen Boudicca and her daughters.

So Queen Boudicca took matters into her own hands. Biding her time, she finally collected an army of 1,00,000 soldiers and marched into Rome. A fierce battle followed. Emperor Nero, the head of the Roman Empire at the time, was forced to give in. But sadly, her triumphs did not last. After many battles, she was finally defeated.

History remembers her as a brave and honourable queen. Even now, there are statues of her and her daughters in London.

14 Bibliography

Agarwal, Deepa. *Rani Lakshmibai: The Valiant Queen of Jhansi*. Puffin Lives Series. New Delhi: Penguin Books India, 2009.

Amazing Women in History. 'Trieu Thi Trinh, the Vietnamese Joan of Arc.' http://www.amazingwomeninhistory.com/trieu-thi-trinh-the-vietnamese-joan-of-arc/.

Ancient History Encyclopedia. 'Boudicca.' https://www.ancient.eu/Boudicca/.

Ancient History Encyclopedia. 'Zenobia.' https://www.ancient.eu/zenobia/.

Aranha, Jovita. 'This Independence Day, Let's Pay a Tribute to the 10 Forgotten Women Warriors of India!' Better India. 15 August 2017. https://www.thebetterindia.com/112037/independence-day-forgotten-women-warriors-india/.

Bodahub. 'Remembering Rani Veeramangai Velu Nachiyar.' http://www.bodahub.com/remembering-rani-veeramangai-velu-nachiyar/.

ILoveIndia.com. 'Rani Lakshmi Bai.' http://www.iloveindia.com/indian-heroes/rani-laxmibai.html.

Important India. 'Brief History of Rani Rudrama Devi.' https://www.importantindia.com/9553/rani-rudrama-devi/.

India Today. 'Remembering the Queen of Jhansi, Rani Lakshmibai.' 18 June 2017. http://indiatoday.intoday.in/education/story/rani-lakshmibai/1/814505.html.

MapsofIndia.com. 'Rani Lakshmi Bai Biography.' http://www.mapsofindia.com/who-is-who/history/rani-lakshmi-bai.html.

MapsofIndia.com. 'Razia Sultana Biography.' https://www.mapsofindia.com/who-is-who/history/razia-sultana.html.

Mocomi.com. 'Rani Laxmi Bai.' http://mocomi.com/rani-laxmi-bai/.

Mudiraja. 'Rani Rudrama Devi of Kakatiya Dynasty.' http://mudiraja.com/mudiraju_queens.html#queen06.

Muvizz. '7 Little-Known Warrior Queens of India.' https://www.muvizz.com/diarydetail?id=89&diary=7-Little-Known-Warrior-Queens-Of-India.